Roses for the Most High

POETRY CELEBRATING THE MYSTICAL
CHRISTIAN PATH

Ronnie Smith

Plenus Gratia Publications

Wildwood, Missouri

Copyright © 2018 by Ronnie Smith.

All rights reserved. No part of this publication may be reproduced, distributed or transmitted, in any form, or by any means, including photocopying, recording, or other electronic or mechanical methods, without the prior written permission of the publisher, except in the case of brief quotations embodied in critical reviews and certain other noncommercial uses permitted by copyright law. For permission requests, write to the publisher, addressed "Attention: Permissions Coordinator," at the address below.

Ronnie Smith/Plenus Gratia Publications
30 Rockwood Forest Valley
Wildwood, MO 63025
www.PlenusGratia.com

Scripture texts in this work are taken from the New American Bible, revised edition © 2010, 1991, 1986, 1970 Confraternity of Christian Doctrine, Washington, D.C. and are used by permission of the copyright owner. All Rights Reserved. No part of the New American Bible may be reproduced in any form without permission in writing from the copyright owner.

Book Cover Design by The Book Cover Whisperer: ProfessionalBookCoverDesign.com
Book Layout © 2017 BookDesignTemplates.com
Interior Illustrations © 2017 by Ronnie Smith

Roses for the Most High/Ronnie Smith. —2nd ed.
ISBN 978-0-9980465-0-1

Contents

Foreword 7
Introduction 9
The Mystic Saints 13
The Mystic Blessed Mother 35
The Mystic Path 55
Footnotes 87
Acknowledgements 89
Author's Note 91

Dedicated to Mother Mary, the Queen of Heaven

Foreword

This is a fine anthology of Christian poetry!

These poems challenge us to transcend our normal patterns of speaking and thinking, even our patterns of listening and noticing, to start us on the path toward participating in a heavenly discourse, requiring the use of higher senses.

Perhaps I can explain it best this way: C.S. Lewis was once asked why he never wrote the counterpart to *The Screwtape Letters*, namely, archangelical advice to a guardian angel about how to lead a person on the path to Heaven. He replied:

> Ideally, Screwtape's advice to Wormwood should have been balanced by archangelical advice to the patient's guardian angel. Without this the picture of human life is lopsided. But who could supply the deficiency? Even if a man—and he would have to be a far better man than I—could scale the spiritual heights required, what 'answerable style' could he use? For the style would really be part of the content. Mere advice would be no good; every sentence would have to smell of Heaven.[1]

What Ronnie Smith is after – and has, in no small measure, achieved – is providing something of the 'answerable style.' The poems here smell of Heaven, to use Lewis' words. That is a great contribution to Christian literature, and no small contribution to the reader's growth in holiness. I have no hesitation recommending it and endorsing it.

Dr. Ed Hogan, Director,
Pontifical Paul VI Institute of Catechetical and Pastoral Studies
Kenrick-Glennon Seminary, Archdiocese of St. Louis

Introduction

A mystical experience, in its most profound meaning, is an existential encounter of a person with God. The Bible bears witness to these divine/human encounters, most notably in Abraham, Moses, the Prophets, Jesus, Mary, the Apostles and Evangelists. Many of these sacred and personal encounters were so profoundly infused with Divine Presence that the persons "divinely touched" later inspired religious communities and, indeed, entire nations to achieve entirely new understandings of God's love for us. Extra-biblical testimony to these sacred encounters are found in the writings of the sages, founders, fathers, luminaries and mystics of every religion whose explicit dynamic is to consciously, freely, and lovingly unite human persons to their Creator.

The author[s] of the Creation accounts in Genesis describe a world, created by God, that was good, harmoniously ordered, and a Garden [Eden] where Adam and Eve, in their naked innocence, walked in the Garden with and spoke directly to God. The inspired truths of these Creation accounts were a radical departure from a surrounding milieu of polytheism and human subjugation to contentious deities and hostile powers of nature. First, in contrast to competing deities and hostile natural forces in need of human sacrificial appeasement, Genesis proclaimed inspired truths that the world and the heavens were created by a benevolent God. Second, Adam and Eve were created in God's own image, sharing a unique, divine closeness. Third, evil entered the universe when the created disobeyed their Creator. This disobedience is symbolized by Adam and Eve eating fruit of that one tree in the entire Garden God expressly forbade them to eat. Adam and Eve, thinking they would become like gods, ate the forbidden fruit. Innocence gone, they covered their nakedness in shame and hid from God. This primeval act of disobedience by the "ones fashioned from the dust of the earth" brought expulsion from the Garden and Divine familiarity -- compounded by pain, suffering, moral disorder, and death.

Mystics throughout the ages, even though profoundly aware of their own failures, have been testament to our primordial closeness to God and to a Creation which, in limitless manifestations, reveals the One whose Love brings into being and sustains all that is.

Ronnie Smith's *Roses for the Most High* is a poetic anthem to Biblical mystics, Christian mystics, and to Ecclesial Sacraments that testify to and continue the Divine/human encounter.

Poetic images and sounds are often such a uniquely personal experience that the passions of the author often fail to ignite the passions of the reader. Poems about mystics and their Divine Encounters present even more challenges because the Words of Love God speaks to an individual soul can be so uniquely personal that often others who hear those same words repeated experience them not wholistically, but rationally. Truly Divine intimacies imbue the whole person - body, mind, heart and soul.

The beauty of Smith's "*Roses*" is their poetic exploration of the Divine/human encounter. His poems about mystical encounter remind us that Creation is a revelation of its Creator, and that, through redeemed innocence and humble love, we, too, are invited continually to re-enter the Garden and to be with God.

Reverend Terrance A. Sweeney

Reverend Sweeney, author of four books and winner of 5 Emmy Awards, holds an M.A. in Communication Arts from Loyola Marymount University, and a Ph. D. in Theology and the Arts from the Graduate Theological Union in Berkeley.

CHAPTER 1

The Mystic Saints

DEVOTION

The Monastic

God is the first exemplar cause of all things.

—Saint Thomas Aquinas [2]

I contemplated mantric shores
and living mist upon the moors
when breath of heather blushed the lea
medieval chants by ancient sea
would reeve galactic jewels that kite
the indigo of endless night

Would I transcend the walls of home
to gust the vast and stellar foam
of countless swirl through dizzy urn
to dusty shell of self return
transformed in tranquil hall of stone
with zeal I held for God alone

Saint John the Baptist

Amen, I say to you, among those born of women there has been none greater than John the Baptist; yet the least in the kingdom of heaven is greater than he.

—Matthew 11:11

But, whom did we expect to see?
As cactus blooms from sun's hot rage,
our desert father fathered me.

His limpid eyes gave true decree—
a river blue through holy sage,
but whom did we expect to see?

Translucent haze on Salt-Dead Sea
Expounds mirage we must engage;
Thus, desert father fathered me.

He planted no apology
With fertile words the ears assuage,
but, whom did we expect to see?

This One drew from a living tree,
whose branch of lightning whacked the age
… as desert father fathered me.

Through truth and water I skip free
to splash the pond beyond my cage,
the whom that I expect to be
since desert father fathered me.

THE LADY IN BLUE

The Lady in Blue

(Venerable Maria of Jesus of Agreda)

Amen, amen, I say to you, whoever believes in me will do the works that I do, and will do greater ones than these, because I am going to the Father.

—John 14:12

You wrote by mystic candle, quill, and well
the clanging hemispheres still sound this knell
of death, which offers, and which takes away
of life, which oft proclaims what no one wants
as resurrection dances its ballet

This toll of truth you rang is bittersweet;
a terrace God descends when we retreat
to scale an inner mount to clear our sight,
for no one hushes evil where it haunts
without the wings to grapple Babel's height

Your prayer transcended prisons of our woes,
for love is our true wealth and always owes,
and when its King and Queen within unite,
this higher union rules the heart's détentes
and taps the royal vats that flood true light

And there the yacht of wisdom glides to seek
Rosetta stones to translate more than Greek,
and at that shore, the castaways of grace
begin to guide through angels and savants
the sacred way without our cyberspace

When first you came of age, you understood
your second life would thrive with womanhood
to nurture nations, farm the lands of time,
and serve as one of Mary's confidantes
to till beneath your veil of love sublime.

To the Mystic Apostle

The revelation of Jesus Christ, which God gave to him, to show his servants what must happen soon. He made it known by sending his angel to his servant John…

—Revelation 1:1

Your exile launched my own
but not to your isle of Patmos
not to visions beyond Pillars of Hercules
where violent seas of silence obliterated
the patter of gab without your door

I sojourned north and south to polar suns
where unrelenting mile is gladiator
and hi-tech czars gnaw his coat of mail
for scavengers seek no savior to forage
the garden of that ice-mad Armageddon

It took two millennia for me to read
your words from the lips of God, yet I
saw where God spoke at the axis of Earth
in glistening crystalline streams that
meditate in waves of frozen rapture

A ripple in the glory of eternity's crisis
as Life battles its own destroyer
a suicide to maintain absolute zero of
eerie beauty, the spectacle its serenity
stages in coliseum of monochrome Trinity

A place to reside inside exile, where
cloud upon cloud exalts and acclaims
the plunder of tundra with ivory javelins
of undying light, scattering gnomes that
taste grit, ash of flesh, and smoke of fire.

Saint Therese of Lisieux

I said, "I will water my plants, I will drench my flower beds." Then suddenly this stream of mine became a river, and this river of mine became a sea.

—Ben Sira 24:29

And for you, little bee, was the dusting of flowers
and the wisdom of fireflies that splashes dim hours,
among reeds of wet roots and the willows of tides,
there was wicker to weave—and the soul's surprise too

For its cloak is a breeze, an endeavor I knew.

And your nook, petite nun, became sky to unfurl
that belittled your self like the tiniest pearl
for the instant we empty and echo subsides
in this castle we yield—so the soul, it flies too

As the clouds do not seize when they sever, I knew

And though you, tiny maid, became smaller to see
through the eyes of The All in the light that is free,
from the point in your journey where silence collides
would the spirit bolt high—for the soul, it cries too

As the sun fills the seas with forever, I knew.

And as you of sweet youth made a whisper your way
and have strewn a true heart with small deeds of the day,
there's a garland of freedom for she who abides
by the death of this self—that the soul defies too

It's a flying trapeze, a flight never I knew.

Desert Fathers, Desert Mothers

But the Lord is in his holy temple; silence before him, all the earth!

>—Habakkuk 2:20

You'd walk away, dropping silk stockings
with harnesses left behind
You carried with charity wooden weights
of society's shackled mind
Through a desert and a desert's fate,
that destroys whatever it will find
You'd rather evaporate and return
as dew for a new day designed.

You rolled the parchment on ascetic stake
and drove it into a cleft behind
Monastic blossoms fume with insignificance
in clear water of mind
Humility is mother of souls,
whose brood includes what Mercy will find
By rope of Will you wielded stones
from mountain crags that God designed.

To isolate delegates soul mates
with death that leaves no burden behind
Your ardent martyrs toted psalms on bare back;
no ballast filled the mind
As Christ sent letters from the kingdom of Light,
so you desired to find
Through stillness, silence, Prayer of Jesus—
as Holy Spirit designed

Lady Julian of Norwich [3]

The fullness of Joy (salvation) is to behold God in everything.

—Lady Julian of Norwich [4]

Indwelling your house next to heaven, a
hooded ponderer was anchorhold to soul;
open dormers, O Julian, invited downpour
from the joy-magician of our Becoming,
who liberates birds of paradise to perch
on washed wood of body, mind, or spirit,
lilting lovesong into the hush of One Who
Dwells in the reflection that never sleeps.

You said, "God made, God loves, and
God keeps," and Who worries not, dearest
Julian; Who left the honey of epic truth
in Mystery's restless creation. Though
deep must be the silence, surely with the
calm of bees, we shall trust retreat into
that hive of Being, should we hunger,
indwelling our house next to heaven.

Saint Teresa of Jesus, of Avila

It is impossible for these two virtues (humility and love) to exist save where there is great detachment from all created things.

—Saint Teresa of Avila [5]

Ago, I climbed interior towers
to view our plains of ancient wars,
to cross the threshold in those hours
and meekly find what love restores,
      a dream that's known for all to dream,
      a distant kingdom it would seem
still beckons us behind these doors

So climb with me as I impart
the lessons I would humbly learn
when Jesus opened up my heart
in ways perfection for Him burn,
      the way that leaves no blame behind,
      that cobbles prayer in roads that wind,
and leads with love at every turn

O comb with me the mystic field,
where earthly powers have no might,
detach with me as we are healed
in Spirit's joys that reunite,
      for whom The Love ensouls is you,
      and soul as hero knows anew
delirium in His delight.

Saint John of the Cross

The Lord said: Now listen to my words: If there are prophets among you, in visions I reveal myself to them, in dreams I speak to them;

—Numbers 12:6

On a cliff we sat and heard your echoes to our distant world. You fell into a cavern of blank sensation, calling backward into your absence within the busy light. You hurtled through dark night, a skydiver ripping through freight of contemplation.

A trail we could not follow while free-falling to a splat against worldly walls, a cessation numb to sadness, as it dares not repeat to us the nights that amount to nothing under street light. Our pulverized blood burns so that virgins carry God's oblation.

Renewed by your rarefied plumb, we tunneled subconscious coal with the dust caking that meditation, aching for harmony among our souls. Pursuit found darkness could equal stillness, and patience to prize virtue, waiting at the grave of the decimation.

Where we were stripped of the rags of every clinging thing. You gave us ample reformation; we, of course, gave you nothing. You, God's saint, who gave up all, suffered scars by a club in the pall of a dungeon steep with the sky of the one and only elation.

Much like incense of precious resin, when our essence comes alive in unpleasant embers of transformation, whose smoke, a purged fragrance of the soul, will lift itself from the world's obsession, from all we continuously scent to cement creation.

Sonnet for Saint Joan of Arc

Then Judith said to them, 'listen to me! I will perform a deed that will go down from generation to generation among our descendants.'

—Judith 8:32

It was your reign in mortal pain for those
you loved, and loved without restraint for good,
That evil be exposed as fear that rose
with flowing vengeance from your rural wood.

When Spirit calls and calls, The Love directs,
so often we refrain from change of life,
And when diversion fails, The Love corrects,
posthaste we take the course of grace through strife.

We sometimes see the tide of love divine,
effulgent waters, no one could have guessed,
poured forward from the mystic heart to shine,
evacuating devils where they wrest.

The Love poured love through Joan that she'd proclaim,
Her sun-hot wreath was pure, and pure its flame.

Saint Hildegard, Rhineland Mystic

Then the prophetess Miriam, Aaron's sister, took a tambourine in her hand, while all the women went out after her with tambourines, dancing;

—Exodus 15:20

Protected by the Bride of Christ,
from youth to Mother-avant-garde,
Your grasp of love for God sufficed
to venture from your German yard

The brilliant Living Light arrived
to let you know where love began,
How ceaseless life forever thrived
and verdant blood through spirit ran

You healed the sick of low estate,
the babe of science you gave breath—
But over poles of frozen plate
I found The White that has no death

You sang the tomes from second sight,
and I from snows where sunlight fails,
I heard the harp of winds that bite,
no trill-melodic nightingales

But brilliant notes both single, true,
are sung in oneness by The White
And penetrate in every hue
the igloo of the inner light

Divine the love that lets us grow
from deep within the soul's abyss,
That Being, whom we barely know,
remembers never ending bliss

And we, for whom the Love of One
will guide the course we cannot chart
Shall see no end to river's run
to row your Rhine within the heart.

Saint Francis of Assisi

But grace was given to each of us according to the measure of Christ's gift.

—Ephesians 4:7

He treasured sun and moon and cast
the seed of God without a care
He sang the breeze of heaven,
even sadness when it stirred the air
He sang to me, as I was fool
for God and swung on spools of light
That I might pluck the poise of combat
captives lost and wars recite

He sang to me, as I was fool
for God and swung on spools of light
I plunged the Sphere of Mercy
finding harmony was beauty's plight
But O! Volcano, creature dear,
and seas shall tout Almighty hand
Whose floes of ice shall serenade
with leis about my Holy Land

There's no volcano, creature dear,
no seas without Almighty hand
That didn't let the mystic speak
of mist or fire The Wisdom planned
The crest of beauty's perfect song,
the ecstasy of ice and sky
No hope, no dream, no painted word,
no soaring bird could ever fly

The crest of beauty's perfect song,
the ecstasy of ice and sky
Untouched by man, the pristine snows
beguile creation's utmost cry
The icy bights were bare as Christ
laid out upon his mother's knee
But joy, the mile, the lap of day
unrolled when I'd forgotten me

The icy bights were bare as Christ
laid out upon his mother's knee
But ice became my hermit son,
who raked the salt to taste the sea
He treasured sun and moon, alas,
the deeds of God that twirl and stare
He sang the breeze of heaven
even sadness when it stirred the air.

Saint Bridget of Sweden

And the whole world sought audience with Solomon, to hear the wisdom which God had put in his heart.

—1 Kings 10:24

Your pilgrim's trail a noble tale acquaints
The throat of arctic winds may groan for saints.

You burned maternal eyes, for love will weep
What cold's privation slows, the ice will reap.

Your travels touched the sick and poor who rove
We hammered frozen air that cyclones wove.

The Pope you sought, assailed by plague's distress
Our foes of ice would light, ignite, fluoresce.

Your Roman prayer would search the pain of Christ
Terrain of stinging snows cannot be priced.

You changed the papal art depicting hell
The Boundless White goes melting from my cell.

The heights that mystics leap your visions beam
We swept the ice tableaux that ever dream.

Your soul would serve as slave for all the lost
A warrior's price is death, if that's the cost.

Saint Faustina

Blessed are the merciful, for they will be shown mercy.

—Matthew 5:7

Besides eternity, to love we flee
to soul and its forest, sower and sown
to pray under mercy's ecstatic tree.

We both left a home in hope to be free
of trappings journey would have us disown.
Besides eternity, to love we flee.

And to follow true joy and love's esprit
I gamboled latitudes of fjord and stone
to play under mercy's ecstatic tree.

She opened doors with humility's key
my door of hope was the nowhere I'd flown.
Besides eternity, to love we flee.

She melted herself in forgiveness' tea.
I strapped on warplanes over black drop zone,
a sleigh under mercy's ecstatic tree.

But World War II she'd have to foresee,
a globe with a zigzag scar I was shown,
Besides eternity, to love we flee
to pray under mercy's ecstatic tree.

Saint Bernadette

She is more blessed, though, in my opinion, if she remains as she is, and I think that I, too, have the Spirit of God.

—1 Corinthians 7:40

Your room, subsumed by ruddy stone
by wood that sizzled, hissed, and popped
where glow of spirit would not die
and would not die within me.

Your room illumined ruddy stone
where hung the lantern you'd adopt
that lit a shrine of rock and sky
of rock and sky within me.

Your room, a broom and ruddy stone
a bed of coals your body propped
and led your soul to purify
and purify within me.

Your room, a tomb of ruddy stone
for dove aloft your sanctum stopped
with dirge to rend with cooing sigh
a cooing sigh within me.

CHAPTER 2

The Mystic Blessed Mother

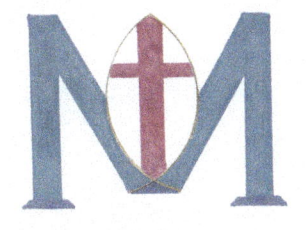

PLENUS GRATIA

Mystery of Mary

…for I wish…thy obedience be that of an angel, and thy love that of a seraphim.

—Venerable Maria of Agreda [6]

The mystery of Mary
conveys her love. Even
the sun, a gilded spark from
just one tub of Wonder's stupor
crackles the black bustle of space,
but no secret of nuclear life has this
shown us, though beams never stream
unknown, to distance conscious infinity

The mystery of Mary
refuses no urchin. Even
our egos, crustaceans we
race to clamp onto a temple
of stone urgent for sky, turn to
study Sanskrit or scribe for ladder
of argot to God, or clamber as fast as
a skeleton rattling from hell, to find her

But mystery of Mary
shall garden souls, pre-
cipitous on an arid acre to
sow. Sudden gushes of joy rise
in us from a well of bliss, as no-
thing less could save us. Moments
like this in her abyss release an axe of
clamor from withering hands awhirl us

My Magnificat

Hear, O kings! Give ear, O princes! I will sing, I will sing to the Lord, I will make music to the Lord, the God of Israel.

—Judges 5:3

A gentle alto carols my true song
and contemplates a labyrinth known as time
for distant is the passage I prolong
a jet to freedom unlike any drone
to love's new country on the winds of Spirit
for eyes that flicker sacred light yet own
the feast of forest orchards blooming near it

But fading into God you feel this 'Who'
who contemplates a labyrinth known as time
for she, who had collapsed, was always you
collapsed between your statues still alive
yet knows the stream that carries us to Source
whose waters white and swift let you arrive
at your frontier, aware without remorse

For God's relentless song sings utter union
and contemplates a labyrinth known as time
until we find it all in one communion
as tranquil fire refines in smoldered earth
our golden butterfly from burnt cocoon
who can't return to time before rebirth
endowed by sun of power, rising moon.

Of the Ten Virtues

Better is childlessness with virtue; for immortal is the memory of virtue, acknowledged both by God and human beings.

—Wisdom 4:1

A pure white lighthouse, lit for me,
that beacons love unknown beyond,
resolves the dark and destiny
of what no other has in store.

Lest any prudent seeker stray
for loss of love unknown beyond,
the best gave utmost every day
for what no other has in store.

And they, the humble, can reflect
The Love of our unknown beyond,
whose looking glass will love perfect
with what no other has in store.

No dialectic faith prevails
to last the long unknown beyond,
the soul will know what love entails
and 'what' no other has in store.

Devotion's trails shall cross the shoal
with bridges to unknown beyond,
no quicksand for the quiet soul
in what no other has in store.

A light and toll we first obey
on highways to unknown beyond,
but when the signposts fall away
we've what no other has in store.

Accumulation pays the rich;
compared to love unknown beyond
its comfort zone is flitting niche
to what no other has in store.

And patience, which we can't outdo
to climb that mount unknown beyond,
becomes the Andes of Peru
for what no other has in store.

This déjà vu that mercy braves
can thrust ascent unknown beyond
if we let go of logic's staves
for what no other has in store.

The knave of sorrows has a mask
that blocks The Light unknown beyond,
and shatters, if at all we ask
for what no other has in store.

Roses on Devotion Road

Undeniably great is the mystery of devotion, Who was manifested in the flesh, vindicated in the spirit, seen by angels, proclaimed to the Gentiles, believed in throughout the world, taken up in glory.

—1 Timothy 3:16

You dropped a rose for me to find
in gospel fathoming, gathering millennia
where you reappear, cropped in the story designed
to forge from quarry and quagmire our true realization
as beauty rests in a humble soul, who tries to serve Light,
who tests the storm to tingle in rainfall from thunderclouds

You dropped a rose for me to find,
drifting on the surface of glimmering day,
for we swam or swapped netherworlds for GloFish
hoping for solitude from salty waves that lap the mind
as beauty rests in a humble soul, who rises from gray-water
where light reveals distortion in aquariums of our self-image

You dropped a rose for me to find,
de-blossoming illusions that we are motherless,
on a road where love exposes all meaningless things
a gift from the King, the Queen, the court of the Saints
as beauty rests in a humble soul for solid eyes of the blind,
to bathe cataracts that disappear in clear mirrors of Eternity

You dropped a rose for me to find
in a tabernacle dripping with mystic nectar,
and behind its lock I plopped in lakes of Presence,
whose pristine pool feeds flocks that wait for our God
as beauty rests in a humble soul, who won't delay return,
to maneuver wasteland planting peace; justice for mankind

You dropped a rose for me to find,
to discover The Lover silence shined
who never stopped hopping like a kangaroo
in devotion's charge of One Way prayer to holiness
as beauty rests in a humble soul, who must ply gravity
if bounding subtle divinity in the reaches of Mary's Rosary.

Canticle

For in the days of David and Asaph, long ago, there were leaders of singers for songs of praise and thanksgiving to God.

—Nehemiah 12:46

My canticle to God extols her love
Bewildering night affixes the wise
Divinity chooses to woo the dove.

Unshakable faith I grip with no glove
So, to wield her Word that no sword defies
My canticle to God extols her love.

To encounter the highest light thereof
My eagle of knowledge to ego dies
Divinity chooses to woo the dove.

Compassion defends all the poor whereof
captivity grows in poverty's guise
This canticle to God extols her love.

The flight to paradise attests hereof
that wind on the sea lifts a cloud that flies
Divinity chooses to woo the dove.

In tugging upslope with rope I can't shove
is hope in the calming fire of her eyes
My canticle to God extols her love
Divinity chooses to woo the dove.

Consecration Day

The Lord said to him: I have heard the prayer of petition which you offered in my presence. I have consecrated this house which you have built, and I set my name there forever; my eyes and my heart shall be there always.

—1 Kings 9:3

Living for you would prove with my life your love

Moreover you, out of Love, are subtle motion at the
origin where I see the unseen; for abandoned to you,
sheer Good will flood degenerate worlds to dredge
the mud-bound toil by flowing Forever's Ever-Now

Dying to prayer in its waves of worship
innocent to refuge in the wash of the holy
vassal to ritual of these tides and seasons
imminent to ponder its wonder and glory
neon to nightmare for perpetual children
ebbing to wax by the moon of the soul

Mindful for you
orphaned for you
torrid for you
humble for you
empty for you
rosy for you

Living for you.

She Chose to Love within the Light

Mary said, "Behold, I am the handmaid of the Lord. May it be done to me according to your word." Then the angel departed from her.

—Luke 1:38

She chose to love within the Light
a peasant girl and youthful wife
a virgin raised by temple rite
despite the sorrows of her life.

How soon the archon angel came
announcing Eden's joy, yet rife
with knowing that her lifelong aim
would heighten sorrows of her life.

Our modern crews of galley slaves
break oars of black and white to knife
a sea of nonconforming waves
to fight the sorrows of this life.

But during storms a moment teems
to mull the love within the strife
this pause of silence God esteems
a light when sorrows color life.

She chose to love within the Light,
the flight of sorrows of her life.

The Grace

Do not press me to go back and abandon you! Wherever you go I will go, wherever you lodge I will lodge.

—Ruth 1:16

If we desire the fruit of sweet illusion
the fruit is fed to fatten calves of gold
but famished camels breed the same confusion
whatever famished camels ache to hold—

But lo! Why weep as forests burn their dead,
whose weeping leaves no leaf upon a tree?
This path can counterpoise where angels led,
for flames of God, of love, we cannot flee!

To timber homes with stilts can hold the slope
and threatened by a mudslide of great weight
shall domes of silence steady us to cope
with beams of peace that brace the entry gate

Inside her house of peace there is a door
to love and only love, forevermore.

The Rosary Weaver

Labor to imitate me with all diligence in all that I did; for…it is this exercise of love, which the Most High is desiring and expecting of thee.

—Venerable Maria of Agreda [7]

This sacred trek of the heart is prairie
For sunsets die and sigh passion's regret
But roses wove a daughter of Mary.

Florid the valleys and plateaus airy!
Wildflower fragrance may hint of Tibet
Though sacred trek of the heart is prairie.

Jewels are attractive, yet, not very
Icy are pearls that our appetites whet
And roses wove a daughter of Mary.

The trail will wind to trial the wary
Gold of the soul is the treasure we get
When sacred trek of the heart is prairie.

Songs of God will the tiny canary
Devotion's prayer will Quiet duet
As roses wove a daughter of Mary.

A million things, less one, we must bury
For of the remains is love's coronet
This sacred trek of the heart is prairie
And roses wove a daughter of Mary.

Deep in the Decades

Then (Elijah) stretched himself out upon the child three times and he called out to the Lord: "Lord, my God, let the life breath return to the body of this child." The Lord heard the prayer of Elijah; the life breath returned to the child's body and he lived.

—1 Kings 17:21-22

Monsoon of prayer and I are one
as mercy falls in soundless rain
to drench where seeded furrows run
in mystery, Mary, my soul.

Entreaties plead as guileless child
when love encounters ego slain,
and walks denuded, undefiled
in mystery, Mary, my soul.

Devotion, faith, and hope create
the flora fuming Truth's domain,
where Jesus' love will ever wait
in mystery, Mary, my soul.

The Nazarene on cross of wood
wrote deeds in blood that will remain,
that God's true love be understood
in mystery, Mary, my soul.

To sit before The Silence awed
can floodlight wisdom once arcane
to share a deathless prayer with God
in mystery, Mary, my soul.

ROSE FOR THE MOST HIGH

The Seven Sorrows

Amen, I say to you, until heaven and earth pass away, not the smallest letter or the smallest part of a letter will pass from the law, until all things have taken place.

—Matthew 5:18

Note: *The letter Yod, the tenth and smallest letter of the Hebrew alphabet, is the primal starting point for all letters. Each has a mystical relationship to creation, depicting how the Hebrew language came directly from God.*

Many elders could prophesy but crow with profanity
distorting innocent rhymes, dreams that rained with mystery
As if woven into the language of life like the tenth letter Yod
Mary felt Simeon's sigh of sorrow's love that weds to God.

Many castles plug the wealth to secure the poor of humanity
Who flee to walls from dragons that devour ever swiftly
As if woven into the language of life like the tenth letter Yod
Mary fled as Herod bled sorrow's love that weds to God.

Many flourish in the institutes to buff tomorrow's urbanity,
Wisdom dozes in caves of a soul, buried by trappings of Me,
As if woven into the language of life like the tenth letter Yod
Mary's son found the stage of sorrow's love that weds to God.

Many a dark timber for cross that crowns hope-filled sanity
can foist a paradox carried within the house of our tragedy,
As if woven into the language of life like the tenth letter Yod
Mary's Jesus toted all of sorrow's love that weds to God.

Many nights we perish in brutal gauntlets of sleepless inanity,
insensitive to the presence of angels who ever face The Holy,
As if woven into the language of life like the tenth letter Yod,
Mary sank, the All stilled, in sorrow's love that weds to God.

Many times we taste a love that dies by callous Christianity.
Yet, everything dies. Even hunger crucifies food completely,
As if woven into the language of life like the tenth letter Yod,
Mary held his body's fate in sorrow's love that weds to God.

Many our strivings that follow the way of matter and its vanity,
Souls reflect Yahweh, often entombed, yet ever shall Be
As if woven into the language of life like the tenth letter Yod
Mary buried Jesus believing sorrow's love that weds to God.

Our Lady of the World [8]

To the clean, all things are clean, but to those who are defiled and unbelieving, nothing is clean; in fact, both their minds and their consciences are tainted.

—Titus 1:15

The gem of Christ became the dawn
whose every day obeys His love
whose prose arose, the highest swan
horizon-long in flight of love

Sublime as night that orbits Sun
she holds the earth in cosmic love
attracting to the Living One
the souls who search this life for love

Her vessel sails the dark in hope
an ark to sate the world with love
She steers a course as slim as rope
a strait to God's utopian love

We scourge our slave, our planet's awe
our world of wonder dies for love
And robot markets stretch the jaw
of profit margins blind to love

Our Lady would for every soul
but those who would the self to love
are those denying Life is whole
are those defying Life and love

The poor, the helpless, we can save
the only famine cries for love
Divine—to share the glut we crave
whose hunger drives our lives from love

Unfailing Mother comes for all
and won't destroy her gift of love
There is no soul that does not fall;
no soul she would not lift to love.

Star of the Imperial Feminine

We saw his star at its rising and have come to do him homage.

—Matthew 2:2

Five, the birth-star rays of The Magi's infant king
Of the Light of our infinite gaze ...

Five, the dimensions aglow through Mary
Of hope, faith, love, life, and grace ...

Five, the wounds that comprehend the Morning Star
Of the enshrined Amen in the Son of Man ...

Five, the portals that light the sensory world
Of sight, smell, touch, taste, and sound ...

Five, the Living Angels irradiating this bountiful world
Of Spirit, Earth, Air, Fire, and Water ...

Five, the realms that brighten under The Helm of the world
Of Soul, Human, Animal, Vegetable, and Mineral ...

Five, the planetary perfections enlightened by her Risen One
Of indestructible gospel ignited by Mary ...

CHAPTER 3

The Mystic Path

THE FIRE OF THE HOLY

Prayer from the Heart

When Solomon had ended his prayer, fire came down from heaven and consumed the burnt offerings and the sacrifices, and the glory of the Lord filled the house.

—2 Chronicles 7:1

The march of our journey in quiet prayer
will elevate love whenever we tear
the mind's cool drifter from court of the heart
to let the true mystic paint the soul's art
with brushes of silence and colors clear ...

But life cannot be a theatre where
we know all the notes, or verse of Voltaire
Our human reverses often restart
the march of our journey ...

In houses of God or temples of air,
we open to love in our heartfelt prayer,
for worship seeks union never to part,
reflecting the love of God in the heart,
Whose everywhere tells of Himself so near
the march of our journey ...

Ritual

You will be to me a kingdom of priests, a holy nation. That is what you must tell the Israelites.

—Exodus 19:6

My cocoon carried me, airborne with all creation, to my lyrical festival of birth, where I awoke to warm hands and lips that sealed me within unbroken life. I gurgled with the cool waters that poured over me, for eternity spoke little else about the origin of rain, after its rising, flying, and falling ... for no matter how we open our ears to words evoked by nature's gestures that silence even angels, we'll see lightning strokes like a cat-o'-nine-tails that shake every subtle world.

I lost my breath to the Arctic Tern flying to the brink of Earth, where I tucked under the wings of the maestro of air, quickened by currents gliding the blue. We were carried by all creation to seasons of one day and one night, and through a frozen portal, where many are left standing and left still. We saw snows which bathe in the rhythms of white rivers for millions of years. This is how we heard its words chanted in canticles that know only purity.

My tepee is a silhouette of three bare trees, who stretch strong angular arms at dawn, inhale their shadows at noon, and vanish on moonless nights. They walk through the forest's aboriginal fog. This sleepless journey begins and ends in mystery when the curtain falls and lifts freely. The daylight finds them glistened, dripping miniscule sounds that spill a universe. We hear their words. They'll be carried in an ark by me, airborne with all creation, to my lyrical festival of death.

The Bronze Voice of God

On that day, "Holy to the Lord," will be written on the horse's bells.

> —Zechariah 14:20

In ancient walls the Gauls of Tours
just aft Saint Martin's sweet noels
but long before the march of Moors
would ring the gong to cull the dells
and led Columban to unseal
the leper sores of royal flings
that yanked the ropes that deeply peal
to fathom bronze and ransom kings.

No longer hid from pagan wars
the Celtic village clapped of bells
to save from stroke of Viking oars
the Lindisfarne and Book of Kells
and tide of day was faithful reel
for Mass and prayer by solemn rings
devoted saints would sink to kneel
to fathom bronze and ransom kings.

The Darkest Angel soon abhors
the faintest Light where evil swells
whose gang of Nazi brutes kept scores
to silence chimes with mortar shells
recasting ancient iron wheel
to smelt the bells for cannon slings
as turret towers bled the zeal
to fathom bronze and ransom kings.

Behind these diabolic doors
angelic horseman, Death, foretells
eternal substance Death restores
through loss of life and somber knells
whose depth within the heart we feel
and in it, Soul has voice of wings
for call of God is not genteel
to fathom bronze and ransom kings

The Glory Be

Blessed are you, O God of our ancestors; blessed be your name forever and ever! Let the heavens and all your creation bless you forever.

—Tobit 8:5

As it was the first fresh moment in the store of cosmic creation

In the beginning the Infinite sired an ubiquitous echo which

Is now and in the future, a memory of all things. Holy Spirit

Ever shall be Muse Divine, whose energy backscatters every

World without end.

Mantle of the Holy Spirit

For the spirit of the Lord fills the world, is all-embracing, and knows whatever is said.

—Wisdom 1:7

This mantle shelters all we dream
and clothes our soul with DNA,
mosaic of this law supreme,
that not one Word shall pass away.

A missionary ferries rain
across the curve of earth by day
to flood with hope the inhumane
that not one Word shall pass away.

Apocalypse, with dreadful look
accosts a kingdom in dismay
an avalanche the nations brook
and not one Word shall pass away.

If birth and death bear love's rosette
unbroken in our cloak of clay
will Mercy purge withal our debt
that not one Word shall pass away.

This mantle shelters all we dream
that not one Word shall pass away

The Flow

Since it is you, Lord, who blessed it, it is blessed forever.

—King David, 1 Chronicles 17:27

Before a sound, The Splendor dwelled to fade
and we from slumber named creation's tree
The Splendor surely rendered every glade
and freed the force of life encaged by sea

Concentric rings in trees have time compressed
in cycles summer-hot and winter-sleeping
aligning with the macrocosm's zest
divining solar winds precisely keeping

A bowing contour softens ruptured land
where deer can dip in shade's recess unseen
and dramatizes stone that plies my hand
to co-create its secret balanced mean

Although The Splendor's flow may show no path
—remembers no beginning, middle, end,
in countless logic rhythms spins Its math
that nature's spewing fractals comprehend.

Elder of the Forest

God looked at everything he had made, and he found it very good.
                              —Genesis 1:31

When I, young mountain, bare and bleak,
a granite shrine with gale for hands
arose from earth, the rare not meek,
I painted skies like colored sands

I gathered hills and spread the plain
and cooled beneath unsullied cloud,
I wedded vales with songs of rain
my morning bride with gown of shroud

My shoulders saplings could not hide
as grasses tippled winds that whined
and covert dens where beasts abide
disclosed my plan for all their kind

Before my bounty, Beauty saw
a palace laced with pale moonlight,
now more the brawn of ore so raw
to stoke your forge for steel and might

When wings of songbirds blaze my stream
and blooms perfume as bees alight
before you soak in blissful dream
recall my love that won't take flight.

Song of Bells

...with pomegranates at the hem and a rustle of bells round about, whose pleasing sound at each step would make (the priest) heard within the sanctuary, a reminder for the people;

—Ben Sira 45:8-9

The angels throng the song of bells
to crack the bolt of our motels
whose walls within that we condone
have tables dressed in foibles known,
Alone, alone, our truth dispels ...

Across the din its tone rappels
the gambits, toys, and sleek cartels
without a word—yet tongues dethrone
the song of bells ...

Like rumbling herd of lithe gazelles
it leaps from towers, guzzles wells
to sweep the spirit's battle zone
(and stop the sap of mobile phone)
Alone, alone, this act foretells
the song of bells ...

The Seven Sacraments

> This is a great mystery, but I speak in reference to Christ and the church.
>
> —Ephesians 5:32

Baptismal gift is ours to claim
no gent's adventure we shall swim
through steaming fog or frozen floes
to whir and flutter Cherubim.

Anointing oil and Christian name
confirm the grace we see as dim,
as soul and not the ego, goes
to whir and flutter Cherubim.

The bread of life the cross would frame
the blood of God by chalice rim,
no other Self from death arose
to whir and flutter Cherubim.

A soul's confession has no shame
when two contrite both sing this hymn,
for we in pious booth compose
with whir that flutters Cherubim.

The flask of life can fail the lame,
but we must tip its frothing brim
with hallowed hands that Jesus chose
to whir and flutter Cherubim.

The cosmic Christ, O Priest, became
your trust in Holy Spirit's vim
in vows to walk the way that knows
the whir that flutters Cherubim.

And chaste as one, will marriage aim
to run magnanimous wonder's whim,
for those who love, will love enclose
in whir that flutters Cherubim.

A Visit with Icons

Let every artisan among you come and make all that the Lord has commanded:

—Exodus 35:10

Under a vault of heraldic stone, at noon
we knelt among spires of your passion-song,
the fiery dye, the fresco of eyes, the scar of
torture in choirs of Light that blaze all time

Your atriums dance cerulean waves,
paint-jagged canvas daggers metal and wood;
and I, ragged in a sanctuary with ten thousand
saints, transfix eternal youth to my ancient God

Foreboding your messianic storm, your mortal city
showered aground with iridescent stars, crosses
born of a crown of thorns explode with the
turbulence of sacred flaming light

Even as Spirit has ever borne the water of life,
So, must every wild river coursing through
dust be holy; we came by fire, without silence,
from terrific thunder and volcanic earth
And fire, from your violence now, of beauty.

Incense Rising

When the priests left the holy place, the cloud filled the house of the LORD ...

—1 Kings 8:10-11

By cloud of sand, dunes buried horizon by a smite of God.
Caravans plowed, balm laden in a blistering blight of God.

By cloud Israel followed whirlwind pillars across alien wilds.
We allowed nations of slavery every day in the sight of God.

By cloud of utterance, Moses decreed for incense all the day
We bowed in halls of modern malls in the spite of God.

By cloud, the Unknowable arrived in the Temple of Solomon.
Aloud, a prayer blurs into hurricanes by the light of God.

By cloud, embers-to-powder reveal a veil amid Eden and us.
A proud word suffocates haze hallowed by the rite of God.

By cloud, swinging censer stirs love from living catacombs.
Snowy shroud to steed and armor a martyr-knight of God.

By cloud, marvel pours from urn of mystery in thanksgiving.
Angels crowd, blown in jollity, unraveling the flight of God.

By cloud, the gloried soul reappears in the gnosis of hearts.
Endowed by blindness, we will purge in the night of God.

By cloud, we unite in the same almighty flame of love.
We vowed to free albino doves, as love is the might of God.

Outdoor Mass at the Convent

Now will I recall God's works; what I have seen, I will describe. By the Lord's word his works were brought into being; he accepts the one who does his will.

—Ben Sira 42:15

You gave us the temple of sky to roam
The purpling clouds for rising dome

The green in the field of the shrub and fern
The incense of grass from sun's slow burn

The song of the nuns in the tender light
And choir of the creatures stars ignite

The flowers, which thirst for our eyes to drink
The lanterns of night as fireflies blink

The Mass is the art that not I compose
By hand we are held in mystic prose.

Holy Water

He is like a tree planted near streams of water, that yields its fruit in season; Its leaves never wither; whatever he does prospers.

—Psalm 1:3

The Word would sing of water's rite
where Sun or Moon forever plays
in pans and plains that splash delight.
The Word would sing of water's rite,
before the roar that worlds incite
through eons, deaf to all but haze,
The Word would sing of water's rite
where Sun or Moon forever plays.

To cross uncharted lakes that glaze
the soul must sail to reach the Light.
The brave invokes its guiding rays
to cross uncharted lakes that glaze
by sacramental waterways
and navigate the ego's night.
To cross uncharted lakes that glaze,
the soul must sail to reach the Light.

Rubaiyat of the Magi (Is our Own)

Therefore, behold, I send to you prophets and wise men and scribes; some of them you will kill and crucify, some of them you will scourge in your synagogues and pursue from town to town, so that there may come upon you all the righteous blood shed upon earth, from the righteous blood of Abel to the blood of Zechariah, the son of Barachiah, whom you murdered between the sanctuary and the altar.

—Matthew 23:34-35

The musk of frankincense was like a fence,
protecting men from evil spirits whence
the Magi's road, mirage of steaming stone,
was known in Palestine for wafting tents.

The Magi's road, mirage of steaming stone,
would tether camels on and on to drone
until the next oasis, water well,
by fevered star the cobalt night had thrown.

Until the next oasis, water well,
if one could stake a space to waylay hell,
we'd see the signs received from God Most High,
to many we are blind and few retell.

To see the signs received from God Most High,
our skeptic mode of logic thunders, Why?
Yet those, the wise, arose from distant lands
to find the Christ that Herod would deny.

Yet those, the wise, arose from distant lands
to help direct the trek through human sands,
They came defying greed with noble prize
we gather when we sift creation's hands.

They came defying greed with noble prize,
and theirs was not a deed for many eyes,
To give our precious gifts away allies
the road to grace when we let Christ arise.

Polar Exile

Has the rain a father? Who has begotten the drops of dew? Out of whose womb comes the ice, and who gives the hoarfrost its birth in the skies?

> —Job 38:28-29

Sub-zero, my inferno
of turquoise skies

and molten, a volcano
to torch my eyes

Crevasses are stigmata
in ice-seared palms

of God's desiderata
for glacial alms

Watcher in the East [9]

And I saw another angel ascending from the rising of the sun, having the sign of the living God;

        —Revelation 7:2, DRA

A ritual of Deity
the ancient dawn of endless birth—
a rhythm of antiquity
the faith of Light to bathe the Earth

A magical incantation
unveils the Whirling Sphere of Fire
A radiant emanation
reveals the Cosmic Lord's attire.

The Holy Trinity

Call to me, and I will answer you; I will tell you great things beyond the reach of your knowledge.

—Jeremiah 33:3

Divinity in Mystery streams forever
whose mounting moments have no sum
Divinity in Life is cosmic lever
facades of God paint sky and slum
Divinity in Mercy will endeavor
throughout Creation's cadenced thrum

What beauty divines without any norms
What power divides and recreates
What love can touch, to love conforms
What joy beholds and rapture elates
What symbol provides, rite transforms
Whatever genius, perception relates
… as galaxies spiral in dizzy swarms

Holy Trinity, innate, transcendent
Holy Trinity, drama resplendent

Advent's Brine of Life

Then the king will say to those on his right, 'Come, you who are blessed by my Father. Inherit the kingdom prepared for you from the foundation of the world.'

—Matthew 25:34

The brine of life appears from cloak of mist
The coming Christ reveals a voyage known
This bitter strait through holy gate of mercy

The starving baby totters toward a fist
The coming Christ reveals what we condone
The brine of life appears from cloak of mist

The wounded soldier, beckoned to enlist
The coming Christ reveals we've war outgrown
This bitter strait through holy gate of mercy

The abject mother, who must dare subsist
The coming Christ reveals the stone we've thrown
The brine of life appears from cloak of mist

The gear of commerce mills our souls for grist
The Christ reveals our 'wheel of fortune' throne
This bitter strait through holy gate of mercy

The love of God can flower and exist
The coming Christ reveals what we postpone
The brine of life appears from cloak of mist
This bitter strait through holy gate of mercy.

Christmastide

The Lord makes poor and makes rich, humbles, and also exalts…

—1 Samuel 2:7

He was sheltered
in the thimble of a womb,
He, through Whom stars again spoke,
through Whom wisdom's ladder and
love's humble lamp
led us back from our black winter,
amnesia in our memory of God

For the coat of God hung
on the swinging door of hope,
the daystar's northbound return
promising summer's feast

Before Immortal Goodness
was wrapped in cloth,
strode in sandals
and left His very Self as the path
to the intimacy of God,
an oscillating sun no more.

The Desert of Lent

Forty years in the desert you sustained them: They did not want; their garments did not become worn, and their feet did not swell.

—Nehemiah 9:21

We run in the desert of Lent
and ruffle its wind through our hair
We fast in rapids of wasteland
for stillness to mingle with air.

Begun in the desert of Lent
is rhythm where baptism thrives
We fast in rapids of wasteland
as ritual touches our lives.

The Son in the desert of Lent,
oasis is He for our hearts
We fast in rapids of wasteland
to drink what Forever imparts.

Undone in the desert of Lent,
the tyrant to time can be bound
We fast in rapids of wasteland
by letting our clock be rewound.

No gun in the desert of Lent
can starve little gods of the self
But fasting in rapids of wasteland
revives our lost youth like an elf.

And won in the desert of Lent,
a present that knows what it's worth
This fast in rapids of wasteland
discovers the soul we unearth.

Lenten Communion

For the water of genuine tears – that is, tears which come from true prayer – is a good gift from the King of Heaven.

—Saint Teresa of Avila [10]

Beads of prayer drip from the hand
wavelets expand shoreless pond
murmurs become the waters of the Word
quarry for sound after language was

It tastes of rain, the breath of the Logos

You whisper—the soul slips its mooring to matter,
let by the billows of fathomless love, lest it
      drown by the Red Sea of sin
      drown by the avalanche of earthen desire
      drown by the holocaust of blind thought
      drown by the chalice of wisdom never drunk
      drown by the shipwreck of apathy,
at once in a marriage to all kingdoms
on the stainless altar of your Anywhere.

Easter Moment at the Cathedral

Consecrate them in the truth. Your word is truth.
                —John 17:17

Polychrome mosaics of The Wondrous
wrap the domes in the robes of ages,
warm wisdom from giants embrace all below
with devotion's initiation of a truth that
is bold, molds, shakes, and stuns this life,

with the truth of the Infinite, who lives in us
with the truth of the Love, who loves us
with the truth of the Messenger, who leads us
with the truth that no sin is worthy of us

to clear the dust of worry from windows of the only 'now'
to contemplate the White Purity, who deigned to die in soot
to holograph sacrifice, resurrection, and certain eternity.

Gates of Grace

Because while the law was given through Moses, grace and truth came through Jesus Christ.

—John 1:17

In the cave of the heart,
before the gift of new Birth, you must die in the dark
then scratch for love's spark for the thatch
of a torch for the sad who sigh in the dark.

You depart at the river of Baptism,
ford and emerge a purified dove
to catch breath from wind, find a patch
to remain aloft and fly in the dark.

To climb the Transfiguration's mount-set-apart,
toss your backpack to the side
and watch prophets through a hatch
of that flaming diamond of the eye in the dark.

The soul imparts no quarter in battle,
marching the hill of Crucifixion
unlatching that very satchel
carried to secure what we tie in the dark.

After fiery darts and a spear,
the Resurrection revives our true temple
dispatching the body-bliss, detaching
the Palace of Versailles in the dark.

In a six-horse cart, the charioteer vanished
in the vest of Ascension, for the reins
he snatched were the coattails that match
our God, Who was nigh in the dark.

Window of Light

My lover is like a gazelle or a young stag. See! He is standing behind our wall, gazing through the windows, peering through the lattices.

—The Song of Songs 2:9

Morning had risen with light through the trees
painting my window from palettes of these:

First was a face of a serious man
Glitter of gold in his dazzling pan
Next was a widow with sadness to speak
Then was a lion to gobble the weak
Next was a fool who had laughed to my face
Blowing his smoke with a puff into space
Then was a demon, a mogul who frowned
Lastly, a boy with a dream I have found.

Mercy [11]

But God, who is rich in mercy, because of the great love he had for us, even when we were dead in our transgressions, brought us to life with Christ (by grace you have been saved).

—Ephesians 2:4-5

Mercy is the pulsing heart of all timeless things.

Faith is the red sun-fire, paused at dawn by prayer of one.

Hope is a white gull, airborne all its life.

Love is the black hole of God.

The Water Carrier

[Jesus] sent two of his disciples and said to them, "Go into the city and a man will meet you, carrying a jar of water. Follow him."

—Mark 14:13

A holy mountain's lively springs
sing joyful songs of God
and clear, the stream of He, who brings
its wondrous waters—love.

And love, like water's fanning rings,
from Jesus overflowed
to drink God's dream, renew all things
with life of boundless trove.

Footnotes

[1] Lewis, C. S. *The Screwtape Letters.* 5th Printing, New York: *MacMillan Company.* 1971. Print. pp. 5-6.

[2] Aquinas, Thomas. *Summa Theologica*, ST I, Q 44, Art. 3, *Newadvent.org.* n.d. Web. 11 Nov. 2018
http://www.newadvent.org/summa/1044.htm

[3] Smith, Ronnie. *"Lady Julian of Norwich."* Dappled Things FEB/MAR 2017, Volume 12, Issue 1, p. 54
http://dappledthings.org/11156/lady-julian-of-norwich/

[4] Lady Julian of Norwich, *Revelations of Divine Love.* Grand Rapids: *Christian Classics Ethereal Library,* 1901. Chapter XXXV. p.69
http://www.ccel.org/ccel/julian/revelations.i.html

[5] Teresa of Avila. *The Way of Perfection.* Garden City: *Image Books.* 1991, Print. p.117

[6] Maria of Agreda. *The Mystical City of God, the Incarnation.* Charlotte: *Tan Books,* 2009, Print. p. 250.

[7] *Ibid.* p. 504

[8] Smith, Ronnie. *"Our Lady of the World."* The Fellowship of the King, thefellowshipoftheking.net. May 6, 2016.
https://thefellowshipoftheking.net/2016/05/06/our-lady-of-the-world/

[9] Smith, Ronnie. *"Watcher in the East."* Hexagon Press, Broadside Vol 1. Nov 2014. https://hexagonpress.com/contra-equus-niveus/

[10] Teresa of Avila. *The Way of Perfection*. Garden City: *Image Books*. 1991, Print. p. 60.

[11] Smith, Ronnie. "Mercy." *Hexagon Press*, December 1, 2014
https://hexagonpress.com/tag/mercy/

Acknowledgements

A special thanks goes to those who assisted and believed in this work. To these professional people I am especially grateful: The Most Reverend Robert J. Hermann, Reverend Nicholas Smith, Dr. Ed Hogan, Sister Maria Battista, O.C.D., Reverend Terrance A. Sweeney, Ph.D., Mr. James Bradley, Ms. Brittany Ham, Mrs. Sandy Doyle, and my editor, Virginia Lieto.

Author's Note

Ronnie Smith grew up in Baltimore, Maryland, where he earned a bachelor's degree at Loyola University, and later studied engineering at the University of Maryland. Colonel Ron Smith, retired from the Air Force after 30 years of service, where he commanded or flew over 1,000 flights in Antarctica. Challenged by extreme winds and temperatures that could drop to minus-75 degrees Fahrenheit, physical and mental endurance were paramount to combat the rigors of prolonged operational stress. He discovered in that world contemplation and divine majesty. His poetry and paintings rest upon the foundation of the underlying wonder of God in humanity and creation. He resides in the Saint Louis, Missouri area and continues to travel and research the lives of the saints, mystics, and the religious cultures of his poetic subjects.

If you have enjoyed reading this book, please post a review, long or short, on Ronnie's website (below), or other book distributor sites. It is very appreciated and helps promote the work.

If you enjoyed reading this book and would like to place a bulk order for your parish, and/or friends, then please note that I offer special discounts on quantity purchases made by corporations, associations, and others. For details or any comments, contact the author at:

Ronnie Smith/Plenus Gratia Publications
PlenusGratiaToday@gmail.com
www.PlenusGratia.com

CPSIA information can be obtained
at www.ICGtesting.com
Printed in the USA
FSHW011728310119
55302FS